408

owning a pet
CAT

Ben Hoare

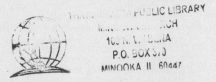

SEA-TO-SEA
Mankato Collingwood London

This edition first published in 2008 by
Sea-to-Sea Publications
1980 Lookout Drive
North Mankato
Minnesota 56003

Copyright © Sea-to-Sea Publications 2008

Printed in China

Library of Congress Cataloging in Publication Data

Hoare, Ben.
  Cat / by Ben Hoare.
     p.cm. -- (Owning a pet)
  Includes bibliographical references and index.
  ISBN-13 978-1-59771-053-4
   1. Cats--Juvenile literature. I. Title. II Series.

SF445.7.H63 2006
636.8--dc22

                     2005056759

9 8 7 6 5 4 3 2

Published by arrangement with the Watts Publishing Group Ltd, London

Series editor: Adrian Cole
Series design: Sarah Borny
Art director: Jonathan Hair
Picture researcher: Kathy Lockley
Illustrations by: Hannah Matthews

The author and publisher would like to thank the following people
and cats for their contribution to the production of this book:

Nat Redfern and Anna Broke, Russell Holdsworth, Jasper and Minnie,
Noodles, Felix the cat.

Acknowledgments:
Alley Cat Productions/Alamy Images 5.
Peter Arnold/Still Pictures 27 b.
Ashmolean Museum, University of Oxford, UK/ Bridgeman Art Library London 6 t.
George Bernard/NHPA 25.
Tim Bird/Alamy Images 14 tr.
Adrian Cole 20 cl. Mary Evans Picture Library 7.
Isobel Flynn/Alamy Images 15.
D. Robert Franz/Alamy Images 26 b.
Robert Harding Picture Library 6 b.
Martin Harvey/Still Pictures 27 t. Paal Hermansen/NHPA 24.
Russell Holdsworth 21 b, 21 t, 28. Juniors Bildarchiv/Alamy Images 8 cr.
Klein/Still Pictures 4, 9 b, 9 t, 13 t, 19 t, 22 c, 22 b.
Yves Lanceau/ N.H.P.A. 16 t.
Elizabeth MacAndrew/NHPA 19 b. Charles Mistral/Alamy Images 10 b.
Ray Moller title page, 11, 17 r, 18 t. Fritz Poelking/Alamy Images 26 t.
Lynne Silver/Alamy Images 14 bl. Robert Slade/Alamy Images 18 b.
Eric Soder/NHPA 17 l. Harald Theissen/Alamy Images 29.

Contents

Pet cats

Cats make excellent pets. They are beautiful, fascinating to watch, and fun to play with. Looking after a cat is not very difficult, but it is a big responsibility.

Cats are one of the most popular types of pet. There are nearly 400 million pet cats all over the world! They come in a wide variety of colors and characters, ranging from elegant pedigrees to playful, mixed-breed pussycats. Unlike their wild relations, for example, lions, tigers and leopards, domestic cats make loveable companions. What's more, their independent and charismatic natures can provide hours of entertainment.

DUTY OF CARE

RSPCA International has outlined five basic rights that should be granted to all pets:

- **Freedom from hunger and thirst**
- **Freedom from discomfort**
- **Freedom from pain, injury, and disease**
- **Freedom to express normal behavior**
- **Freedom from fear and distress**

Cats love to relax, especially in the sun. They are more independent than many pets, but they still need care from their owners.

What a cat needs

Owning a cat is a major commitment because it depends on you for all its needs. These include food, medicine, a safe place to live, and visits to the vet. It will also want lots of attention, especially if it is a kitten. Cats don't have to be walked like dogs, but they do need exercise. Take time to decide if you and your parents have enough time and patience to look after a cat.

"Remember that cats normally live for more than 12 years!"

ARE YOU READY FOR A CAT?

Every year thousands of cats are abandoned because people no longer want them. So make sure you're certain that a cat is the right pet for you. Ask yourself the following questions. You should be able to answer "yes" to each one.

- Is your whole family eager to have a cat?

- Can your family afford to pay for food, vet bills, and other costs such as cattery fees when you go on vacation?

- Do you have time each day to play with, cuddle, and groom a cat?

- Will you be happy if your pet sometimes doesn't want to play when you do?

- Is your home a safe place for a cat to live, with a secure area outside to explore, well away from busy roads?

- Will young children or other pets in your household get along well with a cat?

- Do you know someone who could look after your cat when you are away on vacation?

Cats can usually learn to get along with other pets, if they're introduced at an early age. They may even become best friends!

OBEYING THE LAW

There are laws protecting cats, as with most animals that we keep as pets. It is illegal to harm cats in any way. Animal welfare officers have the power to prosecute cat owners who mistreat their pets. They can impose heavy fines as punishment and may confiscate the animals.

Cats and people

Humans have lived with cats for thousands of years. In the past, some civilizations worshipped cats, while others feared or persecuted them.

Ancient alley cats

Archeologists have found cat bones dating back 6,000–8,500 years among the ruins of ancient towns in Israel, Syria, and Pakistan. It is unlikely that these bones belonged to pets. Instead, the cats probably roamed the streets as wild animals. These "alley cats" must have been popular because they caught the rats and mice that raided grain and other food stores.

Egyptian idols

The first people to tame cats were the Ancient Egyptians, about 3,000–4,000 years ago. Cats were extremely important in Ancient Egyptian society. When they died, their owners would shave off their eyebrows as a sign of respect. The bodies of dead cats were preserved by mummification and buried together in vast tombs. One tomb explored in the nineteenth century contained 300,000 mummified cats. The Ancient Egyptians worshipped several cat gods, including Sekhmet and Bastet, which had cats' faces and women's bodies. The famous Great Sphinx (left) that still stands in Giza, near Cairo, is a carved stone monument with the head of a pharaoh and the body of a big cat—the lion.

"In some parts of the world, black cats are still thought to be bad omens but in Britain they are symbols of good luck!"

East and west

During the Roman Empire (510 B.C.E.–476 C.E.), cats spread throughout Europe. They were highly valued for their mousecatching skills and soon became a familiar sight. Merchants also took cats to Asia and the Far East, where they were popular in palaces and monasteries. In China and Japan, cats became a symbol of well-being. Oriental cats remained slender, with long legs and delicate heads, like their Egyptian ancestors. In the West, however, they gradually developed the stockier build and rounder heads of most common breeds today. European settlers took domestic cats with them to North America in the 1600s and 1700s and to Australia in the 1800s.

In medieval Europe, priests declared that cats had magical powers and worked for witches or the devil. They were accused of being lazy and greedy, and many were beaten or killed.

BEST OF BREEDS

In 1871, the first-ever cat show took place in London, England. It triggered an interest in different coat types and colors, and people began to develop the first cat breeds. Since then, cats have been bred for all sorts of characteristics. Today, there are nearly 50 official domestic cat breeds in the world.

Types of cat

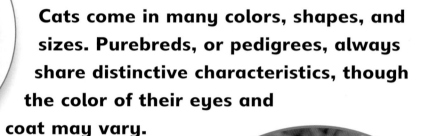

Cats come in many colors, shapes, and sizes. Purebreds, or pedigrees, always share distinctive characteristics, though the color of their eyes and coat may vary.

A SELECTION OF CAT BREEDS

Abyssinian

American Bobtail

Balinese

Birman

Bombay

British Shorthair

Burmese

Chartreux

Colorpoint Shorthair

Cornish Rex

Javanese

Manx

Oriental

Siberian

Somali

Sphynx

SIAMESE

The elegant Siamese originates from Thailand (formerly known as Siam). It has a slim body with long legs and a long neck and nose. Its fur is extremely short and its eyes are bright blue. Siamese cats usually have chocolate-brown, creamy, or whitish-gray coats with darker "points" (ears, nose, and tail).

Character:	Noisy, demanding
Activity:	High
Intelligence:	High
Special needs:	Lots of attention (they love to be around people) and exercise

PERSIAN

The Persian was first brought to Europe from Iran (formerly known as Persia) by traders, although its exact origin is unknown. It has a compact body, short legs, and a bushy tail. Its fur is long, thick, and very soft, and comes in a number of colors. Its rounded face and short nose tend to make the Persian look grumpy.

Character:	Gentle, friendly
Activity:	Low
Intelligence:	Medium
Special needs:	Lots of grooming

MIXED-BREEDS

Most pet cats are usually mixed-breeds— a blend of several different breeds. Their appearance varies enormously, though they often have short hair. They are identified by the color or pattern of their coat.

Tabby .... Dark stripes on body; rings round legs and tail. Various colors, including brown, ginger, and shades of gray.

Tortoiseshell .... Blotches and speckles all over. Either ginger and black, or blue-gray and cream.

Tricolour/Calico .... Tortoiseshell and white.

Colorpoint .... Ears, nose, paws, and tail are all darker than rest of the body.

Solid/Self-colored .. Hairs are all one color from root to tip.

Ticked/Agouti ..... Individual hairs have different bands of color.

Smoked .... Fur is pale with dark tips.

Choosing a cat

When it comes to choosing a cat, you might find you're spoiled for choice. Consider all your options carefully to make sure you end up with the cat or kitten that is right for you.

Cat or kitten?

Kittens are cute and playful, but they are mischievous. They also require a lot of attention as they grow up. Adult cats are generally calmer and easier to look after than kittens. They are often a good choice if you have younger brothers or sisters, or if there are other pets at home. However, cats might find it harder to settle in.

Male or female?

It doesn't make much difference whether you choose a male or a female cat. But it is advisable to have your cat altered (see page 24). This prevents the problem of unwanted kittens. It also improves the temperament of the cat, increases its lifespan, and makes it generally healthier.

Kittens and young cats get really excited when it comes to finding out about the world outside the home. Before you let your cat out, make sure it is fully vaccinated.

"Most cats are happy to spend some time on their own, as long as they're not neglected."

What to look for

Unless you are particularly interested in showing a cat, a mixed-breed is probably a better choice than a pedigree. Mixed-breeds are less expensive and more widely available than purebred cats. What's more, they are usually healthier, less nervous, and easier to care for.

When you're buying a cat, try to find out what its parents are like. In the case of a kitten, visit the litter if you can. Watch how the mother behaves, and also look at the length of her coat. A longhaired cat will shed more hairs around the house, and will need regular grooming.

Cats love to have company, but most also enjoy time on their own. Look at the way a cat behaves before you decide to buy it.

HEALTHY SIGNS
A good choice of cat will have:

- **clean ears and nose**
- **clear, bright eyes**
- **clean, pink gums and tongue**
- **thick, shiny fur with no trace of fleas**
- **a clean rear beneath the tail**
- **a lively, friendly temperament**
- **a keen interest in its surroundings**

BUYING A CAT

Buy a pet cat from an animal shelter or professional cat breeder. Animal shelters look after unwanted pets and normally have many different cats, including kittens. If possible, visit the shelter or breeder several times before you make up your mind. Ask questions about the cat you're interested in. Rescued cats that hiss or seem afraid may have been mistreated in the past—leave these for a more experienced cat owner to adopt. It's best not to buy cats from pet stores, where the animals are often short of space and poorly cared for. For the same reasons, avoid cats offered in newspaper ads, or on websites, even if they are being given away and you feel sorry for them.

Cat environment

Your cat needs a safe environment in which to live. It's a good idea to have everything ready before you bring your cat or kitten home.

Kit list

Bed

Collar and tag

Bowls for food and water

Supply of food

Litter tray and cat litter

Cat carrier

Scratching post

Toys

Brush and comb

A COMFY BED

Pet stores sell a range of cat beds, from plastic baskets to furry igloos. Even a cardboard box can become a cozy nest if you line it with a small blanket or towel. Position the bed in a warm place, such as near a radiator, where your cat won't be disturbed while it sleeps.

Wash your cat's bedding regularly, and check it for fleas.

"It is your responsibility to make sure your home remains a safe place for your cat to live in."

Cats use scratching posts to sharpen their claws. Buy a post to stop your cat from damaging furniture at home.

A CAT-FRIENDLY HOME

Houses can be dangerous places for cats —make sure yours is safe.

DO take special care if you live in an apartment high up or near busy roads. Keep doors shut and consider putting mesh on windows that are open a lot.

DO ensure that you don't have any plants that are poisonous to cats (look on the Internet or ask your vet).

DO make sure that people in your home put away potential hazards, such as poisonous cleaning fluids, sharp knives, etc.

DON'T leave electrical cords lying around. Tuck them away so your cat can't chew on them and get a shock.

DON'T let people in your home turn on the washing machine without first checking your cat hasn't climbed inside.

DON'T leave human food uncovered on tables or units. Your cat could jump up and eat it, which is unhealthy.

DON'T let people in your home display a precious object, such as a favorite vase, where your cat can jump up and accidentally knock it off.

CAT FLAP

Cats love exploring outside, where they can get some exercise and relieve themselves. Ask if a cat flap can be fitted in a door. There are many types available. Then your cat can use it to pop in and out when it wants. Tape or prop the cat flap open to start with to encourage your cat to use it.

Welcome home

Moving into a new home can cause a cat distress. These tips will help you comfort and protect your cat so it settles in happily.

On the move

Cats don't enjoy traveling, so they need special care. Buy or borrow a cat carrier large enough for your cat to stand up in. Cover the base with paper towels, a cloth, or newspaper. Don't feed your cat before the journey in case it throws up, but do take something for it to eat and drink, especially if you're going a long way.

Your cat may be wary of the carrier. Stroke your cat and coax it gently with a toy.

Settling in

For the first few days, keep your cat in a quiet room with the windows closed. Make sure it has plenty of food and water, a snug place to sleep, away from drafts, and a litter tray (see right). The cat will probably be nervous, so don't disturb it too much. Then you can allow it to explore the rest of your home. Introduce your cat to other pets and people gradually, being careful not to make sudden movements or loud noises.

"You can use a strong cardboard box as a cat carrier. Make several square holes in the top and sides to let in plenty of fresh air."

House training

Even if you have a yard, a young kitten will need to be house trained. Put a litter tray on the floor in a corner of your house where it is out of the way. Then fill it with cat litter so that the kitten can scratch around. Take your kitten to the tray as soon as you first bring it home. You may also need to carry it there after meals and when it wakes up, until it learns to go by itself. Clean out the tray every 1 or 2 days, placing the contents in a separate garbage bag. Always wear rubber gloves to do this, and wash your hands afterward.

Cats are very clean animals by nature—they usually scrape soil or litter over their droppings to hide them.

CHOOSING A NAME

Your cat can have a human name or it might suit a more unusual one—it's up to you to decide. Some people name their cat after a place, cartoon character, celebrity, a food, or even a make of car. When you have chosen a name, keep repeating it slowly and gently to your cat. Eventually your cat will learn to recognize the sound.

Cat identity collar

Buy a collar with an identity (ID) tag before you let your cat outside your home. Don't forget: you shouldn't let a kitten out until it is around 12 months old and it has been vaccinated. The ID collar will help to identify your cat if it goes missing. Include your name and telephone number—and keep the details up to date! Check the collar regularly to make sure it fits correctly.

Feeding your cat

Cats need a healthy diet of suitable food. They are carnivores (meat-eaters) and like to hunt they way they would in the wild. But they should eat prepared pet food.

THE RIGHT FOOD

You will find a wide range of cat foods at pet stores and supermarkets. Most of these contain everything your cat needs, including essential vitamins. Look for the words "Complete" and "Balanced." If you have a kitten, buy special kitten food—kittens need more protein and fat than adult cats.

DO read the instructions on the can or package carefully.

DO vary the kind of food you give your cat. Look for different flavors and types.

DO occasionally offer some boneless fish or fresh meat, but make any changes to your cat's diet gradual.

DON'T give your cat sugary, salty, or spicy foods.

DON'T give your cat lots of milk. This can cause stomach upsets, so only offer it as a special treat.

DON'T give your cat chicken bones. It might choke on the small pieces.

If your cat is alone all day, try leaving it some dried food which won't spoil or attract flies. Dried food can also help clean your cat's teeth.

WATER

Cats don't drink huge amounts of water, but it's important that they always have some available. Leave a bowl on the floor near where your cat is fed, and make sure you change the water daily. Cats that eat dried food need to drink more, because they get less liquid from their food.

MEALTIMES

Cats prefer to snack rather than have big meals, so give your cat small amounts of food regularly according to its appetite (see the table below left). Try to feed it at the same times and in the same place each day. Give your cat its own bowl and wash it out after every meal.

Age of cat	No. of daily meals
8 weeks	6
3 months	5
4 months	4
5 months	3
6+ months	2

Cats like to be left alone when they eat. Feed them in a quiet place, away from their bed and their litter tray.

HELPING THEMSELVES

Pet cats eat grass to help their digestion. You may also see them stalking through gardens in search of mice and other small animals. Even well-fed pets hunt, although they might not eat their victims.

FAT CAT

It's unhealthy for your cat to be too fat. If you are worried yours is overweight, ask your vet for advice. You might be overfeeding your cat, or perhaps it is visiting your neighbors for extra treats! Lack of exercise could also be a problem, so make sure your cat has room to run around and explore.

Cat behavior

Cats have their own daily routine and favorite activities. You can learn a lot about the behavior of your cat by watching it go about its business.

Work, rest, and play

Cats enjoy their sleep—they doze in cozy places for much of the day. In the wild they are mostly nocturnal (active at night). Pet cats, too, are often up and about during the night. This is usually when they wander around to inspect and protect their home territory. They may be aggressive toward other cats that come near them, hissing and spitting to warn them off.

Curious cats

Cats always like to know what is going on around them. They love to perch somewhere with a good view, such as a windowsill, chair, or the roof of a parked car. Many cats sit for hours in front of the television! Even when a cat appears to be dozing, it is actually still alert and stays aware of its surroundings. Its sharp senses mean it can detect the slightest sound or movement and is ready to wake up in an instant.

From the top of this wood pile, this cat has a great view of its surroundings. It is less likely to be taken by surprise.

Cat talk

The most common cat sounds are "purring" and "meowing." Purring is a constant humming noise, produced when the cat's voicebox vibrates with breathing. It is usually a sign that the cat is happy, but sometimes cats purr if they're afraid or in pain. Meowing is a more demanding noise. Your cat might meow when it's hungry or just wants attention. Hissing and growling are sounds of anger or fear.

A cat hisses at a rival to warn it away from its territory. If that doesn't work, they may fight.

BODY LANGUAGE

Cats communicate through posture as well as sound. Watch your cat for signs of how it is feeling.

An excited cat

Eyes: wide open
Ears: point forward
Body: back may be arched
Tail: points upward, sways gently
Noise: chirruping or purring

A contented cat

Eyes: shut or half shut
Ears: relaxed
Body: may roll on its back or press its paws to the ground
Tail: relaxed, may sway gently
Noise: purring

An angry cat

Eyes: wide, with narrow pupils
Ears: flattened backward
Body: tense, fur stands on end
Tail: lashes or twitches
Noise: hissing, spitting, or growling

A frightened cat

Eyes: wide, with enlarged pupils
Ears: stick out to side
Body: tense, may slink down low
Tail: upright with puffed-up fur, or hanging between legs
Noise: squealing, growling, or purring

Cat care

Cats are playful animals that usually enjoy human company. Playing is good exercise for your cat, as well as being great fun for both of you.

Playtime

Cats play to practice their hunting skills and also to keep fit. They may leap and pounce on anything that moves! You should play with your cat every day to stop it from getting bored. All sorts of toys are available in pet stores, but many of the things cats play with cost next to nothing. Woolen balls, corks, feathers, and empty toilet paper tubes are all fun to tap and chase. Always watch your cat playing with objects and other toys. Small pieces of string, for example, can be easily swallowed.

Cats are equally as happy with catnip-filled toys (left) as they are with simple toys, such as string.

Going on vacation

When you go away, it is better to leave your cat behind. Arrange for a neighbor or friend to feed it. If possible, they should visit twice a day. Alternatively, you could find a cattery or employ a professional cat sitter. You can find details in local newspapers, at your vet, or on cat websites.

CATS LIKE:

- being stroked, gently scratched, and tickled under the chin
- cuddling on your lap—but only when they are in the mood
- being talked to softly in a soothing voice
- feeling in control

CATS DON'T LIKE:

- being forced to do things
- being teased—this will make them bad-tempered and frightened of people
- being hit or shouted at—this will make them nervous and less obedient in the future
- sudden moves or loud noises

HOW TO HOLD A CAT

There is a correct way to pick up a cat. Reach underneath the cat and hold its chest with one hand. Then use your other hand to scoop up its back legs. Cradle the cat in your arms so that it feels comfortable. Watch out for the cat's claws, and don't pick it up if it is in an aggressive mood.

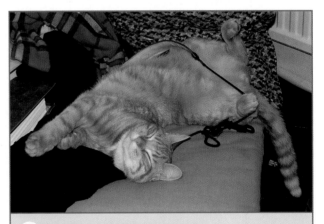

PEACE AND QUIET

Remember that cats enjoy being on their own sometimes. If your cat is asleep, don't wake it up to play games. Cats need more sleep than we do, especially when they are young.

Healthy cats

Pet cats depend on their owners for simple healthcare, such as brushing and giving medicine. Vets look after more serious problems, such as cat flu.

KEEPING CLEAN

Cats keep themselves clean by licking with their tongue, which is rough. This helps remove dirt and loose hair from its fur. The hair collects in its stomach and occasionally the cat has to cough it up as a furball. If you see your cat coughing, this is probably what is happening.

A mother cat grooms her kitten. A kitten has to learn how to clean itself by copying its mother.

GROOMING

Although cats groom themselves, you should still brush your cat once a week with a soft brush. Longhaired cats need to be groomed once a day. Brushing removes loose hair, dirt, and dead skin. It also helps to keep the cat's coat shiny. Always brush in the direction of the cat's fur, from neck to tail—be extra careful around the head and tummy. As you go, stop regularly to remove hair from the brush.

"Visit the vet when you first get a cat or kitten, to check that it's healthy and up-to-date with its jabs."

SIGNS YOUR cat MAY BE unwell

- cloudy or weepy eyes
- itchy or sticky ears
- runny nose
- bad breath
- dull, dried-out fur
- sneezing or persistent coughing
- vomiting or upset stomach
- appetite loss or weight loss
- lack of interest in surroundings
- constant meowing

VISITING THE VET

If you are worried about your cat, call the vet to ask for advice—you may need to take it to the vet's office. Even a healthy cat should go for a checkup once a year. Young kittens need to be vaccinated against serious cat diseases, such as cat flu and feline leukemia. These injections must be renewed yearly with booster jabs.

Regular health checks at the vet will ensure that your cat stays in good health.

FLEAS AND WORMS

Even the cleanest cats catch fleas, which make them itch. Buy some antiflea preparations from a pet store and follow the directions carefully. Another problem cats can suffer from are worms that live inside their bodies. You should give your cat an antiworm treatment every six months or as directed by your vet.

Having kittens

Female cats are some of the best mothers in the animal world—they take great care of their young. Nevertheless, most experts recommend that you shouldn't let your cat have kittens.

Altering

If everyone let their cats breed, the world's cat population would get out of control. Already, thousands of kittens end up as strays, in shelters because they are abandoned, or dead. That's why people are strongly advised to have their pets altered (neutered or spayed). Altering is a simple operation, performed by a vet, to remove part of the cat's reproductive system and prevent it from breeding.

BE RESPONSIBLE

Think before you decide against altering (neutering or spaying):

● Cats that aren't neutered are more aggressive, restless, and likely to run away.

● Your cat could escape and find a mate at any time—not just when you want it to.

● Caring for a mother cat and her young is expensive and a big responsibility.

● Cats have several kittens at once. All need good homes to go to, so leave cat breeding to the experts.

Kittens are born blind. They are totally dependent on their mother and her owner. It is best to leave cat breeding to the experts.

Pregnancy and birth

The average cat's pregnancy lasts for approximately nine weeks. During this time, she will need extra nutrition. If you think your cat is pregnant, ask your vet for advice.

Newborn young

At birth, kittens' eyes are sealed and they can hardly hear. But they use their noses to locate their mother's milk. They suckle for up to eight hours a day and are totally dependent on their mother for warmth and protection.

Kittens feed on their mother's milk. Kittens start to eat solid food when they are 6–8 weeks old.

Leaving mother

Kittens' eyes open within 7–12 days. They can crawl short distances by about two weeks of age and begin to explore farther at about four weeks. At first kittens are clumsy and have shaky leggs, but their confidence soon grows as they start to run and play with their littermates. Kittens should not be taken away from their mother until they are at least eight weeks old.

"An 11-year-old cat is the human equivalent of 60 years old."

CAT FACTS

Pregnancy	9 weeks
Possible litters per year	2–3
Average kittens per litter	3–6
Eats solid food (weaned)	6–8 weeks
Ready for new home	8–12 weeks
First jabs	8–12 weeks
Altering	5–6 months
Fully grown	8–10 months
Average lifespan	12–15 years

Wild cats

Your pet cat is closely related to lions, tigers, and other big cats. Although cats vary in color, shape, and size, they often behave in similar ways.

Meet the family

The scientific name for the cat family is *Felidae*. The family includes 37 species—the domestic cat and 36 different wild cats. Wild cats are found all over the world, except in Australia, where the only felines are domestic cats introduced by humans. Cats live in many different habitats, from snowy mountains to rain forests, marshes, grasslands, and hot deserts.

LARGEST, SMALLEST, FASTEST!

Largest cat
Siberian Tiger (Russia)
Up to 9 ft (2.8 m) long/
660 lb (300 kg) in weight

Smallest cat
Rusty-Spotted Cat (India)
About 16 in (40 cm) long/
2–4.5 lb (1-2 kg) in weight

Fastest cat
Cheetah (Africa): More than
60 mph (96 km/h)—can do
0–56 mph [0–90 km] in 3 secs)

Like many wild cats, Siberian Tigers are severely endangered as a result of hunting and the destruction of their habitat. There may be only 300 to 350 left in the wild.

Natural hunters

Wild cats are predators—they hunt other animals, or prey, for food. Big cats, such as lions, use their strong paws and sharp claws to tackle large prey, including wildebeest and antelope. Smaller species, such as the caracal, eat a variety of prey including rodents, lizards, and birds. All cats have pointed front teeth designed for cutting flesh. Cats' bodies are athletic, muscular, and flexible, which enables them to sprint, leap, and climb when chasing prey. Some cats, including the serval, even swim.

Camouflaged cats

Many wild cats have spots or stripes. These break up the cats' outline so they will blend in with their surroundings. Pet cats tend to have brighter coats than wild cats because camouflage is not as important to them.

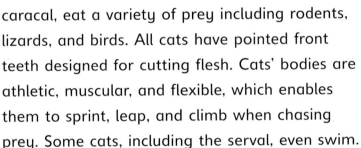

Cheetahs' spots match the shades of light and dark in long grass.

This Iberian Lynx looks similar to some domestic cats. It has a sandy-gray body and looks like a large, pale tabby.

SUPER SENSES

Cats have superb senses of hearing, smell, and sight to locate prey. They can hear sounds four or five times farther away than humans can. Have you noticed how cats' eyes glow in a flashlight beam or camera flash? The ghostly effect is caused by a special layer inside their eyes. This produces a brighter image to help them see better at night.

Losing a pet

Sadly, the typical lifespan of pet cats is about five times shorter than ours. Coming to terms with losing your cat, however it happens, can be very difficult.

FINDING A LOST CAT

Cats' curious natures sometimes cause them to wander off. Do your best to make your house and yard secure, and always encourage your cat to come back to you when it goes outside. If your cat does disappear for longer than normal, ask an adult that you know to help you find it.

- Search your neighborhood, calling your cat's name.

- Ask your friends and neighbors if they've seen your cat.

- Check nearby roads in case there has been an accident.

- Ask if you can put up notices in local shops and at the vet's office.

- Check with animal shelters near your home. Give them details and a photo of your missing cat.

Accidents and illness

You must do everything you can to stop your cat from becoming ill or having an accident. But cats are independent and you can't watch them all the time. If your cat is involved in an accident or becomes ill you should take it to your vet as soon as possible. He or she will be able to assess your cat's condition and discuss the next step with you.

Loss of a friend

If your cat dies suddenly, for example in an accident, your first feeling will be shock; you might not feel anything at all or you might feel very emotional. If your cat dies of old age, it will be less of a shock, but this won't make your feelings easier to deal with. Talk to people around you that you trust. Tell them about what happened and about how you're feeling.

"I felt lonely when Tinker died. I didn't want to forget her so I put her picture in a frame by my bed."

Some people bury their pets in special cemeteries. Others plant trees or flowers to remember their cat by.

Act of remembrance

It is upsetting, but try not to mourn the loss of your cat for too long. Instead, celebrate the good times you had together. You could make a scrapbook of photographs and drawings, or even write a story or poem about your cat. Many people continue to mark the birthday of their cat, even after its death, in a special way.

Saying goodbye

If you've taken good care of your cat, you mustn't blame yourself when it dies —all animals have to die eventually. But there isn't always an easy way to say goodbye. Take time to consider how you and others are feeling. You might have a younger brother or sister who is more upset than you.

AFTER THE DEATH OF A CAT

DON'T rush into buying a new cat. Also, don't accept a new cat from a friend or relative. You need to take time to consider all your options.

DON'T try to replace your cat with one that is exactly the same. Make your decision based on the animal's own characteristics.

DO think about any surviving pets you may have. For example, a dog may not get along as well with a new cat.

DO be aware of how the rest of your family feel. Even if you're coping well, they might not be, especially if you have younger brothers or sisters.

Glossary

Altering: The neutering or spaying of an animal.

Booster jab: A vaccination that renews the effect of a previous one.

Breed: A group of animals within the same species, whose characteristics are passed down from generation to generation. Also means to mate and have offspring, or to organize the reproduction of breeds.

Carnivore: A meat-eating animal.

Catnip: An herb that makes cats playful and relaxed.

Disease: A serious illness; bad health.

Distress: Pain, disturbance, or discomfort usually caused by bad care.

Domestication: The taming of animals to keep them as pets or farm animals.

Endangered species: A species whose numbers are becoming so low it is threatened with extinction.

Habitat: The place where a plant or animal lives, for example a forest.

Medieval: A period of history in Europe from about 400 C.E. to 1500.

Mixed-breed: A cat whose parents are from two or more different breeds.

Mummification: A process by which dead bodies are preserved. It was common in Ancient Egypt.

Neuter or spay: To operate on an animal so it can't have babies.

Pedigree: A pure breed of domestic animal, such as a Siamese cat.

Protein: One of the major food groups.

Species: A group of animals, such as tigers, within the cat family. Species have characteristics in common, distinct from other animals, and can reproduce together.

Vaccination: A medical treatment to prevent a particular disease, often given in the form of an injection. Also called a jab.

Weaning: To feed gradually on solid food instead of milk.

Worms: Parasites that live inside an animal's digestive system.

Websites

If you want to learn more about cats, get more advice, or become involved in animal welfare, there are several helpful organizations you can contact. Your local pet store or vet's office can provide information about groups in your area. The Internet is also a good place to look. Some useful websites are listed here.

www.acfacats.org
The American Cat Fanciers Association (ACFA) is the world's largest registry of pedigree cats and is based in the USA. Its website has a wide range of information on cat breeds and colors, cat shows, and cat care.

www.thecatesite.com
This is one of the largest cat websites on the Internet. A recent count showed that it has more than 5,000 pages. It has cat forums, a cat shop and sections dealing with cat behavior, breeds, care and health as well as lists of recent publications on cats and information about cat suppliers.

www.netpets.com
The website for NetPets®, which is a nonprofit organization, provides a state by state listing of animal rescue shelters. Directories list all the breed clubs and all the varieties of clubs, as well as rescue leagues, shelters, humane societies, and organizations, and includes information about legislation. The site has photo galleries, letters, articles, game rooms for kids, and much more.

More general information on the care, health, and welfare of cats and other pets is available from a number of organizations. These include:

www.rspca.co.uk
The Royal Society for the Prevention of Cruelty to Animals (RSPCA) website has links to RSPCA websites throughout the world. It is full of information about animal adoption, news, care, training and education.

www.hsus.org
The Humane Society of the United States' website offers pet-care guidance to help you maintain a long and rewarding relationship wth your pet. It offers information on issues affecting pets, pet adoption advice, animal shelters, and related news and events.

www.aspca.org
The American Society for the Prevention of Cruelty to Animals website features a wide range of information, from advice about pet care to campaigns fighting cruelty to animals.

www.petwebsite.com
Information and articles on a wide range of pets and petcare options.

Index